The
European
Union

Political, Social, and Economic Cooperation

The European Union

*Political, Social, and Economic Cooperation*

# ITALY

by
Ademola O. Sadek

Mason Crest Publishers
Philadelphia

Mason Crest Publishers Inc.
370 Reed Road, Broomall, Pennsylvania 19008
(866) MCP-BOOK (toll free)
www.masoncrest.com

First printing
1 2 3 4 5 6 7 8 9 10

Library of Congress Cataloging-in-Publication Data

Sadik, Ademola O.
    Italy / by Ademola O. Sadik.
        p. cm.—(The European Union)
    Includes index.
        ISBN 1-4222-0052-3
        ISBN 1-4222-0038-8 (series)
    1. Italy—Juvenile literature. 2. European Union—Italy—Juvenile literature. I. Title. II. European Union (Series) (Philadelphia, Pa.)
    DG467.S24 2006
    945—dc22
                                        2005022625

Produced by Harding House Publishing Service, Inc.
www.hardinghousepages.com
Interior design by Benjamin Stewart.
Cover design by MK Bassett-Harvey.
Printed in the Hashemite Kingdom of Jordan.

# CONTENTS

# THE
# EUROPEAN
# UNION

# ITALY

European Union Member
since 1952

Milan

Verona

Trieste

Torino

Venice

Parma

Bologna

Genoa

Pisa

San Marino

Florence

Livorno

Vatican
City

Pescara

☆**Rome**

Foggia

Bari

Naples

Salerno

*Sardinia*

Taranto

Cagliari

Reggio di Calabria

Messina

Palermo

Catania

*Sicily*

# INTRODUCTION

Sixty years ago, Europe lay scarred from the battles of the Second World War. During the next several years, a plan began to take shape that would unite the countries of the European continent so that future wars would be inconceivable. On May 9, 1950, French Foreign Minister Robert Schuman issued a declaration calling on France, Germany, and other European countries to pool together their coal and steel production as "the first concrete foundation of a European federation." "Europe Day" is celebrated each year on May 9 to commemorate the beginning of the European Union (EU).

The EU consists of twenty-five countries, spanning the continent from Ireland in the west to the border of Russia in the east. Eight of the ten most recently admitted EU member states are former communist regimes that were behind the Iron Curtain for most of the latter half of the twentieth century.

Any European country with a democratic government, a functioning market economy, respect for fundamental rights, and a government capable of implementing EU laws and policies may apply for membership. Bulgaria and Romania are set to join the EU in 2007. Croatia and Turkey have also embarked on the road to EU membership.

While the EU began as an idea to ensure peace in Europe through interconnected economies, it has evolved into so much more today:

- Citizens can travel freely throughout most of the EU without carrying a passport and without stopping for border checks.

- EU citizens can live, work, study, and retire in another EU country if they wish.

- The euro, the single currency accepted throughout twelve of the EU countries (with more to come), is one of the EU's most tangible achievements, facilitating commerce and making possible a single financial market that benefits both individuals and businesses.

- The EU ensures cooperation in the fight against cross-border crime and terrorism.

- The EU is spearheading world efforts to preserve the environment.

- As the world's largest trading bloc, the EU uses its influence to promote fair rules for world trade, ensuring that globalization also benefits the poorest countries.

- The EU is already the world's largest donor of humanitarian aid and development assistance, providing 55 percent of global official development assistance to developing countries in 2004.

The EU is neither a nation intended to replace existing nations, nor an international organization. The EU is unique—its member countries have established common institutions to which they delegate some of their sovereignty so that decisions on matters of joint interest can be made democratically at the European level.

Europe is a continent with many different traditions and languages, but with shared values such as democracy, freedom, and social justice, cherished values well known to North Americans. Indeed, the EU motto is "United in Diversity."

Enjoy your reading. Take advantage of this chance to learn more about Europe and the EU!

Ambassador John Bruton,
Head of Delegation of the European Commission, Washington, D.C.

Italy's peaceful countryside

# 1 THE LANDSCAPE

The Italian Peninsula, easily distinguishable on a map due to its well-known boot shape, encompasses 113,522 square miles (294,020 square kilometers) of land and 2,784 square miles (7,210 square kilometers) of water jutting out from Europe into the Mediterranean Sea. Italy's 1,201 miles (1,932.2 kilometers) of borders are shared with San Marino, Vatican City, France, Switzerland, Austria, and Slovenia. Italy's landscape is primarily rugged terrain, with less mountainous areas mostly near the coasts and around the large metropolitan areas. In fact, about three-quarters of Italy is mountainous or hilly, and the Italian Alps serve as a natural geographical barrier separating Italy from Slovenia, Austria, France, and Switzerland. The highest point in Italy is Monte Bianco de Courmayeur, and the lowest point is the Mediterranean Sea. The Apennine Mountains run through the center of the country.

As a peninsula, Italy is surrounded on three sides by water. The Adriatic Sea to the east, the Ionian Sea to the south, and the Tyrrhenian and Ligurian seas to the west (each of these seas are a part of the larger Mediterranean Sea) surround the mainland of Italy; the Mediterranean Sea is on the east and south of the islands of Sardinia, Corsica, and Sicily. Italy has 1,500 lakes, the largest of which are Garda, Maggiore, and Como, all in the north. The longest river in Italy is the Po, which runs from the Alps to the Adriatic Sea. Another important river, the Tiber, flows from the Apennine Mountains through the capital city of Rome before emptying into the Mediterranean Sea.

## QUICK FACTS: THE GEOGRAPHY OF ITALY

**Location:** Southern Europe, a peninsula extending into the central Mediterranean Sea, northeast of Tunisia
**Area:*** slightly larger than Arizona
  **total:** 116,306 square miles (301,230 sq. km.)
  **land:** 113,522 square miles (294,020 sq. km.)
  **water:** 2,784 square miles (7,210 sq. km.)
**Borders:** Austria 267 miles (430 km.), France 303 miles (488 km.), San Marino 24 miles (39 km.), Slovenia 144 miles (232 km.), Switzerland 460 miles (740 km.), Vatican City 2.0 miles (3.2 km.)
**Climate:** predominantly Mediterranean; Alpine in the far north; hot, dry in the south
**Terrain:** mostly rugged and mountainous, some plains and coastal lowlands
**Elevation extremes:**
  **lowest point:** Mediterranean Sea—0 feet (0 meters)
  **highest point:** Mont Blanc de Courmayeur—15,577 feet (4,748 meters)
**Natural hazards:** regional risks including landslides, mudflows, avalanches, earthquakes, volcanic eruptions, flooding

*Includes Sardinia and Sicily.
*Source:* www.cia.gov, 2005.

## THE CLIMATE

Italy's climate attracts millions of tourists, who come to stay in the beautiful country throughout the year. The climate, due to its many variations, provides something for almost everyone in search of different climactic destinations. The northern parts of the country have an alpine climate, while the southern parts are dryer and hotter. During the summer, northern Italy is warm and experiences plenty of rain, while the central portions of the country are quite humid, and southern Italy is hot and dry. During the winter, the north is cold and damp, with some areas reaching near-freezing temperatures, but the south has a mild winter, with temperatures rarely dipping below 50°F (around 10°C).

Italy is nearly surrounded by the Mediterranean.

Italy's rocky coast

## Natural Disasters

Natural disasters in Italy range from mudslides and avalanches to volcanic eruptions (Mount Vesuvius and Mount Etna are two well-known active volcanoes in Italy), environmental activities that result directly from the largely mountainous terrain found in the nation. Sadly, pollution poses a significant threat to the lands and waters in which Italy takes pride.

## Wildlife and Plants

Numerous forms of wildlife are present in Italy, but many have become endangered by overhunting. Foxes, wolves, black bears, and deer are present in many remote areas, and swallows, grouse, and falcons also live in these wild regions. In the seas, sardines, sharks, tuna, and anchovies are common. The whale population is also making a comeback due to determined efforts by ecological societies. Increased awareness of environmental issues has prompted many Italians to reserve, preserve, and conserve. Many national parks have been established to create safe havens for animals that would otherwise have limited habitats.

In 2001, scientists at Italy's University of Teramo successfully cloned a European mouflon, one of the smallest breeds of wild sheep in the world. The mouflon's native habitats are Corsica, Sardinia, and Cyprus, and the mouflon population in Europe is near extinction. Because of the success of the cloning, renewed efforts to determine the benefits of cloning endangered animals to preserve populations are under way.

Highways cross the Italian Alps, going in and out of tunnels and across bridges.

Italy's best-known floral icon is the olive tree, with 15 million of these trees growing across the country's landscape. The Romans spread olive trees across the entire peninsula, and the oldest olive trees in Italy are over 2,000 years old. Recently, many have been stolen by tree thieves who sell them on the black market to wealthy European collectors. Because of the sheer number of olive trees, the Italian government is finding it difficult to act against the removal of what some consider part of Italy's heritage.

Olive trees aren't the only things that have fallen prey to the black market. Mushrooms, ***truffles***, and bounty from Italy's botanical gardens are also quite popular on the underground market.

The city of Venice, with its ancient canals, has many stories to add to Italy's long history.

# 2 ITALY'S HISTORY AND GOVERNMENT

CHAPTER

Italy has a rich history that stretches back to *prehistoric* times. During the **Neolithic** period, small agricultural-based communities replaced the hunter-gatherers of the Paleolithic and Mesolithic periods. Settlers from the east introduced the use of metal to the peninsula during the Bronze Age. With the arrival of these newcomers came distinct regional identities, which developed by 1000 BCE when the use of iron became prevalent.

Indo-European-speaking tribes began to arrive in what is now known as Italy late in the Neolithic period. These tribes, such as those speaking Latin and Venetic, settled in the peninsula but would be forced to wait their turn to exert any extensive influence over their neighbors. The **indigenous** non–Indo-European Etruscans extended a wide influence over the central portion of the peninsula and even dominated and ruled many Latin communities. Later Roman historians note that the Etruscans ruled the city of Rome for many years, and it was only after they were overthrown and

## DATING SYSTEMS AND THEIR MEANING

You might be accustomed to seeing dates expressed with the abbreviations BC or AD, as in the year 1000 BC or the year AD 1900. For centuries, this dating system has been the most common in the Western world. However, since BC and AD are based on Christianity (BC stands for Before Christ and AD stands for *anno Domini*, Latin for "in the year of our Lord"), many people now prefer to use abbreviations that people from all religions can be comfortable using. The abbreviations BCE (meaning Before Common Era) and CE (meaning Common Era) mark time in the same way (for example, 1000 BC is the same year as 1000 BCE, and AD 1900 is the same year as 1900 CE), but BCE and CE do not have the same religious overtones as BC and AD.

expelled that the Latin tribes began to forge what would eventually become one of the greatest empires the world has ever known.

## THE BIRTH AND GROWTH OF ROME

The mythical legend of the city of Rome's founding states that Romulus and Remus, twin sons of a Vestal Virgin raped by Mars, the god of war, founded the city, and Romulus became its first king. This account is clearly laden with mythological exaggeration, but whatever the true origin of the city, after the expulsion of their Etruscan overlords, Rome began to emerge as the premier Latin settlement, and its inhabitants began socially and militarily dominating their Latin cousins around them. The Latins lived in Latium, a plain on the western coast of the Italian Peninsula, and were loosely associated with one another in what was known as the Latin League.

As Rome grew increasingly powerful, it began to exercise a great deal of dominion over the other cities in the league. Tension rose as the rest of Latium began to fear a Roman plan to rule the entire plain and beyond. The Latin War of 340–338 BCE pitted

Medieval buildings are still standing throughout Italy.

Rome against its Latin kinsmen and resulted in a Roman victory, dissolving the Latin League and creating a senatorial government in Rome. Rome now dominated all Latin-speaking peoples and began to pose a threat to the other tribes of the peninsula.

The Etruscans, Gauls, Samnites, and other people on the peninsula engaged Rome in a series of wars between 326 BCE and 290 BCE. Known as the Samnite Wars, there were three in total, and although Rome suffered a great deal of defeats, it also displayed a great deal of resilience, eventually defeating all who wished to challenge her authority and ruling all of Italy except the Greek cities in the south and the territory of the Gauls to the north. The subsequent Pyrrhic and Punic wars and other conflicts also found Rome victorious, leading to the defeat of her last true rival, Carthage. Rome now had the beginnings of a consolidated empire.

Julius Caesar was the greatest ruler of the Roman *republic*. A brilliant general and politician, he extended and solidified Roman rule into the Iberian Peninsula, Britannia, and the main portions of the remainder of Europe. During these events, Rome was still a republic ruled by the Senate, many of whom believed Caesar was growing too powerful. In 44 BCE, a group of sen-

The Colosseum is one of Italy's most famous reminders of the Roman Empire.

ators murdered the popular Caesar, and after a period of civil unrest, his nephew and adopted son Octavius marched on Rome and forced the Senate to name him consul. He would eventually become the first Roman emperor, after first sharing leadership with Julius Caesar's general Marc Antony and Marcus Lepidus. Under Octavius, who was renamed "Augustus," the Roman Empire expanded to rule most of the known world. This empire would last for hundreds of years until internal strife and external threats from Germanic tribes weakened the once great empire.

## THE FALL OF ROME

Because of political corruption, selfish emperors, and other undermining internal factors, Rome's power began to decline. The generals of the formerly invincible army cared more for their villas and estates than their legions' well-being and success. Weakened armies meant the barbaric Germanic tribes no longer needed to live in fear of repercussions of rebellion. They began to revolt, and without competent generals abroad or a stable emperor at home (from 186 CE to 286 CE, thirty-seven different emperors ruled, and twenty-five of those were assassinated), the empire plunged into disarray. The movement of gold into the coffers of Rome slowed as Rome stopped conquering new lands, but wealthy Romans continued to spend gold on luxury items. Because of this outflow of precious metal, less gold was available for use in minting coins, and the value of minted money dropped. This caused inflation, as merchants raised the prices of their goods. All these causes, and more—such as the split of the empire into the Roman and Byzantine empires—led to the sacking of Rome in 476, during the reign of Romulus Augustus. The Roman Empire was no more.

## MEDIEVAL ITALY

After the fall of Rome, the Byzantine Empire in the East continued the legacies of both Rome and Greece, but control of Italy was eventually lost to the invading Lombards. Italy once again splintered into ethnic strongholds. The Lombards, a Germanic tribe, ruled an extensive portion of the peninsula, until the **papacy** invited the Franks (another Germanic tribe) to invade Italy in order to restore land that the Church had lost. This began the rule of the Holy Roman Empire (under Charlemagne) in Europe. Around this time, Arabs from North Africa conquered Sicily, but they were eventually expelled by the Normans, who established a kingdom on the small island.

Strong **city-states** began to arise in Italy during the Middle Ages. Florence, Milan, and Venice, among others grew powerful through trade, and Italy was effectively splintered into regional rule. Strong and wealthy families in the city-states began to rule and gain influence. In 1494, two years after Italian Cristoforo Colombo (Christopher Columbus) discovered the New World, Charles VIII of France invaded Italy, ending the wars between rival city-states and beginning a long period of foreign rule. The Hapsburg Dynasty brought most of Italy under control, and when the dynasty was divided between Emperor Ferdinand I and King Phillip II of Spain, Phillip inherited Italy. In the early 1700s, Austria **annexed** Italy in the War of the Spanish Succession (1701–1714). Small parts of Italy began gaining independence from foreign rule, but the nation remained fragmented into separately ruled regions.

## UNIFICATION OF ITALY

Foreign rule made the dwellers of the Italian Peninsula desire freedom. Revolutions by the Carbonari, a radical group, were **quelled** by the Austrians, as were the Revolutions of 1848, in which the king of Sardinia declared Italy free and created a constitution. In 1859, France and England saw an Austrian defeat as favorable to their political interests. Sardinia led the battle for Italian independence against Austria with the help of Giuseppe Garibaldi, who led his "Redshirts" to the southern part of the peninsula and captured it, then, showing his true patriotism, handed it over to King Emmanuel II of Sardinia. The Kingdom of Italy was formed officially in 1861.

The new nation had many internal problems. Its citizens thought of themselves not as Italians, but identified more with the region of their birth and ancestry. The country was in debt, and the pope refused to recognize the new nation, furious over the seizure of papal lands. The northern portion of the country developed to a greater extent than the southern portion. Crime and social activism increased as the poorer south seemed stuck in its misery. The people were for the most part poor and illiterate, and the nation had nothing in terms of international prestige or recognition. In an attempt to gain status as a colonial power, Italy foolishly attacked the stronger African nation of Ethiopia and was embarrassed on an international level as they were defeated soundly in the 1890s. It apparently failed to learn its lesson as Italy went on to declare war on Turkey over the North African nation of Libya in 1911. During World War I, Italy joined the Allies only to suffer staggering losses of men and machines during the course of the war. The postwar failure of the Allies to provide lands that Italy had been promised on joining the Allied war effort led to a generally disgruntled Italian population, laying down the foundations for Benito Mussolini and fascism to take control of the nation.

## THE RISE OF FASCISM

Benito Mussolini began the fascist movement in Italy. His "Blackshirts," a squad of thugs who terrorized those whose views differed from Mussolini, helped him gain strength in the troubled nation. King Victor Emmanuel III named Mussolini prime

Italy's past and present are mixed together in the village of Portofino.

minister in 1922, and within several years, the nation had been transformed into a military state by the new regime. In 1935, Mussolini sent troops back to Ethiopia to compensate for the embarrassing military fiasco of the 1890s, and the following year Italian troops were sent to Spain to aid Francisco Franco in the Spanish Civil War.

German dictator Adolf Hitler formed the Rome-Berlin Pact in 1936, and both dictators continued to **_satiate_** their aggressive land-seizing propensities as Hitler annexed Alsace-Lorraine and the Sudetenland, while Mussolini added Albania to Italy's territory. The English prime minister Neville Chamberlain and his French allies continued to

Italy's modern politics are visible on a Genoa street wall.

**appease** the two obvious threats, and the result of this was the outbreak of World War II, when Hitler attacked Poland, with Mussolini joining the war on the German side several months later.

## WORLD WAR II

During World War II, Italy's meager conquests were generally overshadowed by the stronger successes of the German *blitzkrieg*, or lightning war. The overall incompetence of Italy's army was an embarrassing contrast to Rome's past military prowess. The Allies invaded Italy in 1943, and Mussolini was expelled to a puppet government in the northern part of the nation after King Victor Emmanuel III forced him to resign. Mussolini was captured and executed by communist partisans during the final stages of the Allied expulsion of the German army from Italy.

## POSTWAR ITALY

The monarchy was abolished in 1946 and a new republican constitution was drafted. The United States gave a great deal of aid to Italy as a part of the **Marshall Plan**, and because of this, the Italian economy grew considerably. Industrial expansion and economic growth resulted in a

### THE TOWER OF PISA

One of Italy's most recognizable sights is the Tower of Pisa. The bell tower of the city's cathedral, it sits in Pisa's *Campo dei Miracoli*, Field of Miracles.

Work began on the tower in 1173 and continued for almost two hundred years, with a couple of long interruptions. For many years, it was believed that the leaning was a "design element," but it is now known that the tower was meant to stand erect. The leaning began during the building, and many construction mechanisms were tried to prevent the tilt. Nothing worked. Efforts are still under way to stop the inclination from progressing. Today's efforts are focused on the subsoil beneath and around the tower.

Even if the tower was straight, it would still be one of the most impressive sites in the country. But, there wouldn't be the traditional photographs of tourists holding up the tower to keep it from falling.

higher standard of living for the average Italian citizen. However, the 1970s saw a return to labor unrest and political agitation. Extremist groups seemed to be on the rise until the mid- to late 1980s under the premiership of Bettino Craxi, when the economy made a recovery.

## THE ITALIAN GOVERNMENT

Today, the Italian form of government is a republic. Universal **suffrage** has been granted to

The leaning Tower of Pisa

all citizens over the age of eighteen, but for senatorial elections, the minimum age requirement is twenty-five years of age. The executive branch of the government consists of the president, the Council of Ministers, and the prime minister, who is also the president of the Council of Ministers. The Italian parliament and fifty-eight regional representatives form an electoral college that elects the president for a seven-year term. The president in turn nominates a prime minister, who must be approved by parliament. He also nominates a Council of Ministers to preside over and be approved by the president.

The *parlamento*, or parliament, is comprised of the *Senato della Repubblica*, or Senate, and the *Camera dei Deputati*, or Chamber of Deputies, in a **bicameral** configuration. There are a number of senators for life, a classification all former presidents are placed in. The senators serve five-year terms, as do legislators in the Chamber of Deputies.

The judicial branch of the government is composed of the *Corte Costituzionale*, or Constitutional Court. This court has five judges appointed by the president, five elected by the parliament, and five elected from Supreme Courts.

President Carlo Azeglio Ciampi was elected on May 13, 1999, and Prime Minister Silvio Berlusconi was elected on June 10, 2001. There are myriad political parties in the government with many parties forming coalitions with other parties, creating party conglomerates such as the Daisy Alliance, which was formed by the Italian Popular Party, the Italian Renewal Party, the Union of Democrats for Europe, and the Democrats.

> **Fast Facts About the Tower of Pisa**
>
> The Tower of Pisa is 180.4 feet (55 meters) tall, weighs approximately 14,500 tons, and has 294 steps.

The Italian Riviera along the Mediterranean Coast attracts many tourists.

# 3 THE ECONOMY

Since the unification of Italy in 1861, the northern regions of Italy have always enjoyed greater prosperity and industrial viability than the southern regions. The southern, more agricultural region lacks the industry and private companies that the north has always possessed. Italy's natural resources include coal, zinc, and marble, and the surrounding presence of water has allowed the fishing industry to grow.

In 2004, Italy's **gross domestic product (GDP)** was US$1,609 billion. The 2004 per capita GDP, the country's total GDP divided by the total population, was US$27,700. The main sources of Italy's GDP are 68.9 percent from the **service sector**, 28.8 percent from industry, and 2.3 percent from agriculture.

The employment of Italy's labor force of 24.27 million reflects the importance of the service sector and industrial sector to Italy's economy. Approximately 63 percent of the workforce are employed in the service sector, and 32 percent work in industry. Only 5 percent of the workforce are employed in agriculture-related occupations.

Italy's major industries include tourism, chemical production, textiles and design of fine apparel, and motor vehicle production. The predominant agricultural products generated in Italy are beef, dairy products, fruits and vegetables, and fish.

Some of Italy's main trading partners are Germany, France, and Spain. Among Italy's lucrative exports are luxury cars; Italy is a world leader in their production. Car companies

## QUICK FACTS: THE ECONOMY OF ITALY

**Gross Domestic Product (GDP):** US$1.609 trillion

**GDP per capita:** US$27,700

**Industries:** tourism, machinery, iron and steel, chemicals, food processing, textiles, motor vehicles, clothing, footwear, ceramics

**Agriculture:** fruits, vegetables, grapes, potatoes, sugar beets, soybeans, grain, olives; beef, dairy products; fish

**Export commodities:** engineering products, textiles and clothing, production machinery, motor vehicles, transport equipment, chemicals; food, beverages and tobacco; minerals and nonferrous metals

**Export partners:** Germany 13.7%, France 12.1%, Spain 7.3%, UK 6.9%, Switzerland 4.1%

**Import commodities:** engineering products, chemicals, transport equipment, energy products, minerals and nonferrous metals, textiles and clothing; food, beverages, and tobacco

**Import partners:** Germany 18.1%, France 10.7%, Netherlands 5.8%, Spain 4.7%, Belgium 4.4%, UK 4.3%, China 4.1%

**Currency:** euro (EUR)

**Currency exchange rate:** US$1 = €.82 (August 1, 2005)

*Note:* All figures are from 2004 unless otherwise noted.
*Source:* www.cia.gov, 2005.

Fishing plays a part in Italy's economy.

such as Ferrari, Alfa Romeo, Maserati, Fiat, and Lancia are exported to almost every country in the world. These expensive cars have given Italy a reputation for fine things over the years; many of these car companies date back to the early 1900s.

Most of Italy's energy needs must be met by imports; Italy produces only 79,460 barrels per day (bbl/day) of oil, while consuming 1.866 million bbl/day. The nation also produces 15.49 billion cubic meters of natural gas and consumes 71.18 billion cubic meters of natural gas. Much of

Italy's terraced vineyards

the oil and gas required for Italy is imported. Italy has 1,058 miles (1,703 kilometers) of crude oil pipeline, 1,225 miles (2,148 kilometers) of petroleum product pipeline, and 12, 055 miles (19,400 kilometers) of natural gas pipeline.

Since the construction of its first railroad in 1839, Italy has developed its rail system into one of the most impressive in Europe. Most rail stations in Italy are famous for their beautiful architecture. Italy has international rail links to France, Austria, Switzerland, and Slovenia and, in 2005, began plans for possibly building an underwater subway system from Sicily to Tunisia.

With 406,797 miles (654,676 kilometers) of highway, over-the-road transport of goods is easily accomplished. Italy has many harbors and ports along its coastline, and 136 airports, making ship and air transport viable options as well.

Italy's budget has been, in some aspects, in need of attention in the past few years. The budget breached the 3 percent deficit maximum that the European Union (EU) allows, and the high taxes levied on Italy's citizens have done nothing to reduce the external debt of $913.9 billion.

The sea has an important role in Italy's culture.

# 4 ITALY'S PEOPLE AND CULTURE

Many different ethnicities and cultures are represented among the 58 million inhabitants of Italy. This is in part due to the almost perpetual foreign rule that the nation has been under for much of its history. Recent immigration has added to the country's rich diversity. The majority of people are Italian, but there are clusters of German-Italians, Greek-Italians, French-Italians, and Slovene-Italians. Most ethnic groups are bilingual, speaking Italian along with their native languages. (The Greek-Italians in the southern regions and Sicily are descendants of the Greeks who in ancient times migrated to and colonized the portions of Italy that became known as Magna Grecia; they speak Griko, a language descending from Greek.) The island of Sicily's inhabitants are ethnically a mix of Italians, Greeks, Phoenicians, and Arabs; some also have Norman, Spanish, and Albanian ancestry. Sicilian is a distinct **Romance language** spoken by most of its inhabitants, although it is spoken less and less as a first language, since the Italian spoken in public schools takes precedence among the youth.

A large influx of recent, mostly illegal immigrants from the continent of Africa is increasing the ethnic diversity of Italy. Although mainly from North African nations, there is an increasing number of Italians of Sub-Saharan origin living primarily in large cities such as Rome. The North African immigration is increasing Italy's Muslim population.

The persecution of Kurds in Turkey in recent years has caused an increase in Kurdish migration to Italy. Italy has been criticized by other EU member states such as Germany on its seemingly open-door policy toward unauthorized Kurdish immigration. These EU member

## QUICK FACTS: THE PEOPLE OF ITALY

**Population:** 58,103,033
**Ethnic groups:** Italian; includes small clusters of German, French, and Slovene Italians in the north and Albanian Italians and Greek Italians in the south
**Age structure:**
    *0–14 years:* 13.9%
    *15–64 years:* 66.7%
    *65 years and over:* 19.4%
**Population growth rate:** 0.07%
**Birth rate:** 8.89 births/1,000 pop.
**Death rate:** 10.3 deaths/1,000 pop.
**Migration rate:** 2.07 migrant(s)/1,000 pop.
**Infant mortality rate:** 5.94 deaths/1,000 live births
**Life expectancy at birth:**
    *Total population:* 79.68 years
    *Male:* 76.75 years
    *Female:* 82.81 years
**Total fertility rate:** 1.28 children/born woman
**Religions:** Predominately Roman Catholic with mature Protestant and Jewish communities and a growing Muslim population
**Languages:** Italian, German, French, Slovene
**Literacy rate:** 98.3% (2003 estimate)

*Note:* All figures are from 2005 unless otherwise noted.
*Source:* www.cia.gov, 2005.

states claim that illegal Kurdish immigration to Italy, when coupled with the open borders among all EU nations, results in a wave of illegal Kurdish immigration to other EU nations, immigration the other nations may not be able to accommodate.

Most of Italy's population is Roman Catholic. However, the Protestant, Jewish, and Muslim communities are small but growing.

## THE ARTS

Italy has a rich history of art, architecture, and literature. In the fourteenth century, the Renaissance began in Italy. Beginning in the city of Florence in northern Italy, the Renaissance spread to the remainder of Italy and then to the rest of Europe, effectively ending the Dark Ages. The Renaissance,

Italians are politically active.

An Italian woman pedals home with her shopping.

which means "rebirth" in French, was a period in which new ways of thinking and new artistic and literary methods of expressing those new thoughts were developed. Italy holds an illustrious place among those countries that produced well-known Renaissance thinkers. Works from influential thinkers such as Machiavelli, author of *The Art of War* and *The Prince*, and art from the likes of Michelangelo, who created the famous nude statue of the Hebrew King David and the ceiling **frescoes** of Rome's Sistine Chapel, are renowned worldwide. The futuristic designs of Leonardo da Vinci, whose notebooks even contain plans for a rudimentary helicopter, and his world-famous artworks including *Mona Lisa* and *The Last Supper*, were also among the products of the Italian Renaissance.

Italy is widely known as the birthplace of opera. Traditionally, most opera is performed in Italian. Opera was exported to other nations in Europe, and the result is many non-Italian composers have written operas. However, Italians such as Giuseppe Verdi and Giacomo Puccini remain favorites of opera lovers worldwide.

Another Italian contribution to music is the invention of the pianoforte, or piano, some time in the late 1600s by Bartolomeo Cristoforo of Florence. The piano would soon develop into the primary instrument of composers in the latter part of the Baroque period, lasting through the Classical period. Some of the most beautiful pieces in the European musical repertoire are written for piano.

The Italian influence extends to music notation. All performance instructions are written in Italian. For example, the notation instructing the individual playing the music to play loudly is *forte*, the Italian word for loud.

Today's Italian youth listen to a variety of musical genres. Italian rap and hip-hop are enjoying a considerable growth in popularity as Italian artists decide to venture into these wildly popular

## Did You Know?

You can't get Parmesan cheese or Chianti wine just anywhere, and many countries are urging the passage of international laws to prevent attaching names such as Parmesan or Chianti to cheese and wine produced outside a particular region. To be truly Parmesan cheese, it must be produced in the Parma region of Italy. Chianti wine is produced only from grapes grown in the Chianti region of Tuscany.

American genres for themselves. Rock and roll is another import of American origin, with Italian stars such as Zucchero enjoying immense popularity not only in Italy but in the rest of Europe also. Traditional folk artists also are popular among all ages in Italy, and Patchanka, an Italian mix of punk, reggae, and rock, often with politically charged lyrics, is another frequently heard musical genre.

## CUISINE

When it comes to food, Italy's reputation for **gastronomic** delights is world famous. Italian contributions to the world of cuisine include pizza and pastas such as spaghetti and linguine. Italian breads and soups are known for their heartiness. Wine and cheese are other popular Italian exports. The country is also home to a wide selection of sausages. Two of the most famous are bologna, a seasoned sausage of mixed meats originating in the Italian city that shares its name, and salami, another seasoned sausage.

## RECREATION AND LEISURE

Italians love sports, both as spectators and participants. Association football, known as "football" in much of the world and as "soccer" in the United States, is the most popular sport in Italy. In Italy, football is a religion, each stadium is a Mount Olympus, and every player is a god. Italy has

Passersby in busy Genoa

won the World Cup, the world championship, three times.

Italy has developed a cultural reputation as a world leader in fine clothing and luxury cars. Italian designers such as Gucci, Fendi, Prada, Salvatore Ferragamo, and Dolce and Gabanna lead the world in producing the **opulent** clothing and accessories worn by the rich and famous. Italian manufacturers such as Maserati and Ferrari dominate the luxury car field, each producing luxury cars with features once thought possible only in science fiction.

## HOLIDAYS

Because most of the Italian population is Roman Catholic, many of the holidays and festivals that are a major part of Italian culture are based in Catholicism. Holidays and festivals, such as Christmas, Epiphany, and St. Stephens Day, are all celebrated in accordance to Roman Catholic tradition.

People around the world love pasta and tomato sauce . . . Gucci designer bags . . . and the art of da Vinci and Michelangelo. Italy's food, art, and style all enrich the entire world.

Venice's skyline

# 5 THE CITIES

I taly is for the most part a rural nation, with its towns and villages nestled among rolling hills and mountainous landscape. There are, however, many urban hubs where the majority of Italy's industrial development and demographical diversity can be found. Cities such as Rome, Milan, Naples, and Turin are growing yearly in infrastructure and development.

# Rome

The capital of Italy, and its largest city, is Rome. An ancient city dating back thousands of years, Rome is full of history, landmarks, and tourist attractions. Many areas of the city date back to Roman times and are preserved to this day. With 2.6 million inhabitants, the city of Rome can be quite cramped in some places. Italian cities are known for their small, narrow streets, and for the most part Rome is no exception. The historical sites range from ancient tombs, the Forum, and the Colosseum to medieval buildings. The seat of the Roman Catholic Church is Vatican City, which is an enclave within the city of Rome. St. Peter's Basilica in the Vatican is a popular tourist attraction.

Rome is quite accessible, with several airports bringing tourists into the city. Leonardo da Vinci International Airport, Giovan Battista Pastine International Airport, and Aeroporto dell'Urbe all can be used to enter the city of Rome and the surrounding metropolitan districts.

# Milan

Milan is Italy's second-largest city with 1.3 million people living within the city limits. Another historical city, Milan has several notable Roman monuments, such as the Columns of San Lorenzo and other ruins of its past Roman glory. The city's main function in Italy's modern society and economy is as a financial center and a leader in the

The Vatican dominates Rome.

An aerial view of Milan

bustling fashion industry of Italy. The city, accessible to tourists through its Nalpensa and Linate airports, is home to designers Versace, Dolce and Gabbana, and Giorgio Armani. The Quadrilatero, the city's exclusive shopping area, is a popular stop for many tourists for its unique mix of history and fashion.

## NAPLES

Naples, with a population of 1.04 million people, is Italy's third-largest city. It is the traditional birthplace of pizza and home to the oldest opera house in Europe, the Teatro di San Carlo. The city also has one of Europe's oldest aquariums, which can be found in La Villa Comunale, an area that was formerly a royal park. Museo Archeologico Nazionale Napoli, the National Archeological Museum of Naples, has a large collection of Roman artifacts such as the Farnese Marbles, classical marble statues made by Roman sculptors of the Roman emperors, and figures in nature. It also houses replicas of ancient Greek statues that have long been lost or destroyed. Naples, home to extensive Roman catacombs, also has the Museo Nazionale di Capodimonte, which contains many works by Michelangelo and Raphael.

## TURIN

The city of Turin has 921,485 residents, and with three rivers (the Po, Dora Riparia, and Stura di Lanzo) running through the city, and major indus-

Italy's Alps draws visitors from around the world.

tries such as the Fiat car manufacturer's main factory within city limits, Turin is the most important city in northwestern Italy. The host city of the 2006 Winter Olympics, it is Italy's fourth-largest city and, as much of the rest of Italy, is rich in history. The **Shroud of Turin** is housed in the Cathedral of St. John the Baptist, and Museo Egizio holds the second-largest collection of ancient Egyptian artifacts in the world. Home to many royal palaces and historical buildings that were named World Heritage Sites in 1997, the city of Turin's close proximity to the Italian Alps brings another group of yearly visitors to the area. The famous Italian football club, Juventus, calls the city of Turin its home, and many football enthusiasts from across the globe enjoy watching the world-class football Juventus has to offer.

The EU flag

# 6 CHAPTER

# THE FORMATION OF THE EUROPEAN UNION

The EU is an economic and political confederation of twenty-five European nations. Member countries abide by common foreign and security policies and cooperate on judicial and domestic affairs. The confederation, however, does not replace existing states or governments. Each of the twenty-five member states is *autonomous*, but they have all agreed to establish some common institutions and to hand over some of their own decision-making powers to these international bodies. As a result, decisions on matters that interest all member states can be made democratically, accommodating everyone's concerns and interests.

Today, the EU is the most powerful regional organization in the world. It has evolved from a primarily economic organization to an increasingly political one. Besides promoting economic cooperation, the EU requires that its members uphold fundamental values of peace and **solidarity**, human dignity, freedom, and equality. Based on the principles of democracy and the rule of law, the EU respects the culture and organizations of member states.

## HISTORY

The seeds of the EU were planted more than fifty years ago in a Europe reduced to smoking piles of rubble by two world wars. European nations suffered great financial difficulties in the postwar period. They were struggling to get back on their feet and realized that another war would cause further hardship. Knowing that internal conflict was hurting all of Europe, a drive began toward European cooperation.

France took the first historic step. On May 9, 1950 (now celebrated as Europe Day), Robert Schuman, the French foreign minister, proposed the coal and steel industries of France and West Germany be coordinated under a single supranational authority. The proposal, known as the Treaty of Paris, attracted four other countries—Belgium, Luxembourg, the Netherlands, and Italy—and resulted in the 1951 formation of the European Coal and Steel Community (ECSC). These six countries became the founding members of the EU.

In 1957, European cooperation took its next big leap. Under the Treaty of Rome, the European Economic Community (EEC) and the European Atomic Energy Community (EURATOM) were formed. Informally known as the Common Market, the EEC promoted joining the national economies into a single European economy. The 1965 Treaty of Brussels (more commonly referred to as the Merger Treaty) united these various treaty organizations under a single umbrella, the European Community (EC).

In 1992, the Maastricht Treaty (also known as the Treaty of the European Union) was signed in Maastricht, the Netherlands, signaling the birth of the EU as it stands today. **Ratified** the following year, the Maastricht Treaty provided for a central banking system, a common currency (the euro) to replace the national currencies, a legal definition of the EU, and a framework for expanding the

The EU's united economy has allowed it to become a worldwide financial power.

EU's political role, particularly in the area of foreign and security policy.

By 1993, the member countries completed their move toward a single market and agreed to participate in a larger common market, the European Economic Area, established in 1994.

The EU, headquartered in Brussels, Belgium, reached its current member strength in spurts. In

CHAPTER SIX—THE FORMATION OF THE EUROPEAN UNION

© BCE ECB EZB EKT EKP 2002

© BCE ECB EZB EKT EKP 2002

© BCE ECB EZB EKT EKP 2002

© BCE ECB EZB EKT EKP 2002

The euro, the EU's currency

1973, Denmark, Ireland, and the United Kingdom joined the six founding members of the EC. They were followed by Greece in 1981, and Portugal and Spain in 1986. The 1990s saw the unification of the two Germanys, and as a result, East Germany entered the EU fold. Austria, Finland, and Sweden joined the EU in 1995, bringing the total number of member states to fifteen. In 2004, the EU nearly doubled its size when ten countries—Cyprus, the Czech Republic, Estonia, Hungary, Latvia, Lithuania, Malta, Poland, Slovakia, and Slovenia—became members.

## THE EU FRAMEWORK

The EU's structure has often been compared to a "roof of a temple with three columns." As established by the Maastricht Treaty, this three-pillar framework encompasses all the policy areas—or pillars—of European cooperation. The three pillars of the EU are the European Community, the Common Foreign and Security Policy (CFSP), and Police and Judicial Co-operation in Criminal Matters.

## QUICK FACTS: THE EUROPEAN UNION

**Number of Member Countries:** 25
**Official Languages:** 20—Czech, Danish, Dutch, English, Estonian, Finnish, French, German, Greek, Hungarian, Italian, Latvian, Lithuanian, Maltese, Polish, Portuguese, Slovak, Slovenian, Spanish, and Swedish; additional language for treaty purposes: Irish Gaelic
**Motto:** *In Varietate Concordia* (United in Diversity)
**European Council's President:** Each member state takes a turn to lead the council's activities for 6 months.
**European Commission's President:** José Manuel Barroso (Portugal)
**European Parliament's President:** Josep Borrell (Spain)
**Total Area:** 1,502,966 square miles (3,892,685 sq. km.)
**Population:** 454,900,000
**Population Density:** 302.7 people/square mile (116.8 people/sq. km.)
**GDP:** €9.61.1012
**Per Capita GDP:** €21,125
**Formation:**
- Declared: February 7, 1992, with signing of the Maastricht Treaty
- Recognized: November 1, 1993, with the ratification of the Maastricht Treaty

**Community Currency:** Euro. Currently 12 of the 25 member states have adopted the euro as their currency.
**Anthem:** "Ode to Joy"
**Flag:** Blue background with 12 gold stars arranged in a circle
**Official Day:** Europe Day, May 9

*Source:* europa.eu.int

The European Community pillar deals with economic, social, and environmental policies. It is a body consisting of the European Parliament, European Commission, European Court of Justice, Council of the European Union, and the European Courts of Auditors.

The idea that the EU should speak with one voice in world affairs is as old as the European integration process itself. Toward this end, the Common Foreign and Security Policy (CFSP) was formed in 1993.

## PILLAR THREE

The cooperation of EU member states in judicial and criminal matters ensures that its citizens enjoy the freedom to travel, work, and live securely and safely anywhere within the EU. The third pillar—Police and Judicial Co-operation in Criminal Matters—helps to protect EU citizens from international crime and to ensure equal access to justice and fundamental rights across the EU.

The flags of the EU's nations:

top row, left to right
Belgium, the Czech Republic, Denmark, Germany, Estonia, Greece

second row, left to right
Spain, France, Ireland, Italy, Cyprus, Latvia

third row, left to right
Lithuania, Luxembourg, Hungary, Malta, the Netherlands, Austria

bottom row, left to right
Poland, Portugal, Slovenia, Slovakia, Finland, Sweden, United Kingdom

## ECONOMIC STATUS

As of May 2004, the EU had the largest economy in the world, followed closely by the United States. But even though the EU continues to enjoy a trade surplus, it faces the twin problems of high unemployment rates and **stagnancy**.

The 2004 addition of ten new member states is expected to boost economic growth. EU membership is likely to stimulate the economies of these relatively poor countries. In turn, their prosperity growth will be beneficial to the EU.

## THE EURO

The EU's official currency is the euro, which came into circulation on January 1, 2002. The shift to the euro has been the largest monetary changeover in the world. Twelve countries—Belgium, Germany, Greece, Spain, France, Ireland, Italy, Luxembourg, the Netherlands, Finland, Portugal, and Austria—have adopted it as their currency.

## SINGLE MARKET

Within the EU, laws of member states are harmonized and domestic policies are coordinated to create a larger, more-efficient single market.

The chief features of the EU's internal policy on the single market are:

- free trade of goods and services

- a common EU competition law that controls anticompetitive activities of companies and member states

- removal of internal border control and harmonization of external controls between member states

- freedom for citizens to live and work anywhere in the EU as long as they are not dependent on the state

- free movement of **capital** between member states

- harmonization of government regulations, corporation law, and trademark registration

- a single currency

- coordination of environmental policy

- a common agricultural policy and a common fisheries policy

- a common system of indirect taxation, the value-added tax (VAT), and common customs duties and **excise**

- funding for research

- funding for aid to disadvantaged regions

The EU's external policy on the single market specifies:

- a common external **tariff** and a common position in international trade negotiations

- funding of programs in other Eastern European countries and developing countries

## COOPERATION AREAS

EU member states cooperate in other areas as well. Member states can vote in European Parliament elections. Intelligence sharing and cooperation in criminal matters are carried out through EUROPOL and the Schengen Information System.

The EU is working to develop common foreign and security policies. Many member states are resisting such a move, however, saying these are sensitive areas best left to individual member states. Arguing in favor of a common approach to security and foreign policy are countries like France and Germany, who insist that a safer and more secure Europe can only become a reality under the EU umbrella.

One of the EU's great achievements has been to create a boundary-free area within which people, goods, services, and money can move around freely; this ease of movement is sometimes called "the four freedoms." As the EU grows in size, so do the challenges facing it—and yet its fifty-year history has amply demonstrated the power of cooperation.

Europe is proud of its "bright idea," a union with economic and political power.

The EU believes that it can use its power to act as a "lighthouse" for the rest of the world.

# KEY EU INSTITUTIONS

Five key institutions play a specific role in the EU.

## THE EUROPEAN PARLIAMENT

The European Parliament (EP) is the democratic voice of the people of Europe. Directly elected every five years, the Members of the European Parliament (MEPs) sit not in national **blocs** but in political groups representing the seven main political parties of the member states. Each group reflects the political ideology of the national parties to which its members belong. Some MEPs are not attached to any political group.

## COUNCIL OF THE EUROPEAN UNION

The Council of the European Union (formerly known as the Council of Ministers) is the main legislative and decision-making body in the EU. It brings together the nationally elected representatives of the member-state governments. One minister from each of the EU's member states attends council meetings. It is the forum in which government representatives can assert their interests and reach compromises. Increasingly, the Council of the European Union and the EP are acting together as colegislators in decision-making processes.

## EUROPEAN COMMISSION

The European Commission does much of the day-to-day work of the EU. Politically independent, the commission represents the interests of the EU as a whole, rather than those of individual member states. It drafts proposals for new European laws, which it presents to the EP and the Council of the European Union. The European Commission makes sure EU decisions are implemented properly and supervises the way EU funds are spent. It also sees that everyone abides by the European treaties and European law.

The EU member-state governments choose the European Commission president, who is then approved by the EP. Member states, in consultation with the incoming president, nominate the other European Commission members, who must also be approved by the EP. The commission is appointed for a five-year term, but can be dismissed by the EP. Many members of its staff work in Brussels, Belgium.

## COURT OF JUSTICE

Headquartered in Luxembourg, the Court of Justice of the European Communities consists of one independent judge from each EU country. This court ensures that the common rules decided in the EU are understood and followed uniformly by all the members. The Court of Justice settles disputes over how EU treaties and legislation are interpreted. If national courts are in doubt about how to apply EU rules, they must ask the Court of Justice. Individuals can also bring proceedings against EU institutions before the court.

## COURT OF AUDITORS

EU funds must be used legally, economically, and for their intended purpose. The Court of Auditors, an independent EU institution located in Luxembourg, is responsible for overseeing how EU money is spent. In effect, these auditors help European taxpayers get better value for the money that has been channeled into the EU.

## OTHER IMPORTANT BODIES

1. European Economic and Social Committee: expresses the opinions of organized civil society on economic and social issues

2. Committee of the Regions: expresses the opinions of regional and local authorities

3. European Central Bank: responsible for monetary policy and managing the euro

4. European Ombudsman: deals with citizens' complaints about mismanagement by any EU institution or body

5. European Investment Bank: helps achieve EU objectives by financing investment projects

Together with a number of agencies and other bodies completing the system, the EU's institutions have made it the most powerful organization in the world.

## EU MEMBER STATES

In order to become a member of the EU, a country must have a stable democracy that guarantees the rule of law, human rights, and protection of minorities. It must also have a functioning market economy as well as a civil service capable of applying and managing EU laws.

The EU provides substantial financial assistance and advice to help candidate countries prepare themselves for membership. As of October 2004, the EU has twenty-five member states. Bulgaria and Romania are likely to join in 2007, which would bring the EU's total population to nearly 500 million.

In December 2004, the EU decided to open negotiations with Turkey on its proposed membership. Turkey's possible entry into the EU has been fraught with controversy. Much of this controversy has centered on Turkey's human rights record and the divided island of Cyprus. If allowed to join the EU, Turkey would be its most-populous member state.

The 2004 expansion was the EU's most ambitious enlargement to date. Never before has the EU embraced so many new countries, grown so much in terms of area and population, or encompassed so many different histories and cultures. As the EU moves forward into the twenty-first century, it will undoubtedly continue to grow in both political and economic strength.

Italy acts as a leader in the European community.

# ITALY IN THE EUROPEAN UNION

Italy is a founding member of the EU, and has held the presidency of the EU eleven times. As an original member, Italy holds an important position in the EU. In 2005, Italy ratified the new constitution for the EU, but the rejection of the constitution by

France and the Netherlands has put the future of the new constitution in doubt; the assent of all member nations is necessary for the proposed constitution to take effect. The assent of all member states governments before an international organization can act is a concept known as inter-governmentalism; the opposite policy would be supranationalism, in which the representatives of the member states make decisions. The EU uses both of these methods in its actions, and some EU nations generally support one over the other. Italy supports a supranational approach, along with several other European nations, notably France.

The EU constitution had considerable support in Italy. The Italian parliament's lower chamber approved the treaty in January of 2005, and then the Senate ratified it by a resounding 217 to 16 vote.

One of the primary goals of the constitution is to prevent the EU from **_encroaching_** on the rights of member states other than in areas where the members have given their rights away. Critics of the constitution say that the EU can act in so many areas that this clause does not mean much, but supporters of the constitution say it will act as a brake to protect member states from a too powerful EU. At the same time, however, the constitution provides for a greater role for the EU in more aspects of life. In some areas, the EU will have exclusive competence, in others a shared competence, and in still others, only a supporting role. The constitution also changes the way the EU reaches a decision, making votes dependent on a majority rule rather than a unanimous vote.

Portofino, a resort village on the Italian Riviera

Italians use small trucks to conserve gas.

Supporters of the constitution believe that if all twenty-five members had to agree, nothing would ever be accomplished. The constitution does, however, provide for an "emergency brake," whereby a country outvoted on an issue could take its case to the European Council. The voting system outlined in the constitution replaces the old one under which countries got specific numbers of votes. Critics of the old system objected that Spain and Poland had too many votes; they believe that the new method will allow for a fairer balance between large and small countries. The new constitution will also allow for the president to serve for two and a half years, rather then six months as is currently the case. Countries like Italy that support the constitution believe this will allow the president to be a more permanent figure with greater influence and symbolism and the power to be more effective with greater continuity—but since the president will be subject to the council, the powers of the post will still be limited. Not everyone agrees, however.

Other key points in the constitution include:

- The commission, the body that proposes and executes EU laws, will consist of one national from each member state for its first term of five years. After that it will be slimmed down to "a number of members . . . corresponding to two-thirds of the number of Member States," unless the European Council, acting unanimously, decides to alter this figure. It is felt that the current commission is too big with not enough jobs to go round.

Italy's road toward the future looks optimistic.

- The EU will for the first time have a "legal personality," and its laws will trump those of national parliaments. By having a legal personality, the EU will be able to enter into international agreements.

Italy is a strong **proponent** of the EU and European integration. The Italian parliament, which for the most part generally represents the political leanings of the Italian public, ratified the proposed constitution without any trouble. However, support of the euro is weak. Many Italians and other Europeans believe that prices of common goods like food rose sharply after the continent-wide introduction of the euro. Many supermarkets and other businesses in Italy began accepting the Italian lire, the former currency of Italy, in 2005. Some Italian politicians want the country as a whole to return to the lire, dropping the euro completely.

Inflation, economic woes, and troubles that have already left Italy on the receiving end of harsh **castigation** from the EU. Italy, along with Portugal and Greece, have all been **censured** by the EU for changing the listed amount of money borrowed to comply with the union's borrowing guidelines. Many financial analysts predict that this may be the start of the decline and eventual rejection of the euro as an international currency.

Italy has played an important role in European and world history for centuries. Its location, heritage, and position in the EU will only allow it to grow more influential in years to come. Italians have added diversity and a rich culture wherever they have gone, and Italy has left the legacy of Rome and the influence of Christianity on each nation of the world.

# A Calendar of Italian Festivals

Italians celebrate festivals of cultural and religious origins. Each festival is an opportunity to enjoy good food and the company of family and friends.

**January: New Year's Day**, or *Capodanno* in Italian, is celebrated on January 1. These festivities are usually marked by consumption of alcohol and the singing of traditional folk songs with good friends and family. Many Italian cities sponsor New Year's Day celebrations in central locations within the city. **Epiphany**, *Epifania* in Italian, is celebrated on January 6. Those of the Eastern Orthodox faith celebrate this festival, which represents the birth of Jesus, more than others. Many people celebrate the "Twelve Days of Christmas," the twelve days between December 25 (Christmas Day) and January 6 (Epiphany).

**March/April: Easter Sunday**, *Pasqua* in Italian, is officially the first Sunday after the first ecclesiastical full moon on the same day of or any time after the vernal equinox (the vernal equinox is March 21). Easter is celebrated in Italy according to traditional Roman Catholic tradition, with observance beginning on Holy Saturday, the day before Easter Sunday, and continuing until Easter Monday, the day after Easter Sunday. **Easter Monday**, *Lunedì di Pasqua* is also a national holiday in Italy. Another holiday celebrated in April is **Anniversary of Liberation**, *Liberazione* in Italian. This holiday celebrates the end of World War II in Europe in the year 1945.

**May:** May 1 is celebrated as **Labor Day**, or *Festa del Lavoro* in Italian.

**June:** June 2 is **Republic Day**, *Festa della Repubblica* in Italian. This holiday is a commemoration of the birth of the Italian Republic in 1946, when a referendum removed the former monarchy and replaced it with a democratically elected government. This holiday is one the Italians hold very dear.

**August: Assumption Day**, *Assunzione* or *Ferragosto* in Italian, is August 15. A Roman Catholic holiday, this is a celebration of the Roman Catholic belief that the Virgin Mary's body was taken up into Heaven at the end of her time on Earth. Parades and festivals are among the events that mark this public holiday in Italy.

**November:** November 1 is the festival of **All Saints' Day**, known as *Ognissanti* in Italian. This Roman Catholic holiday is in honor of all the saints and martyrs in Christian tradition, and is celebrated with a vigil and an octave in honor of the dead.

**December:** December 8 is the celebration of **Immaculate Conception**, called *Immacolata Concezione* in Italian. This honors the Roman Catholic belief that the Virgin Mary was born and lived her entire life free of sin. Also celebrated in December is **Christmas Day**, or *Natale* in Italian, a holiday that in Christian tradition honors the birth of Jesus Christ. Christmas in Italy is celebrated beginning the night before on Christmas Eve, with most observant Italians going to mass, and the worldwide tradition of exchanging gifts on Christmas Day is also observed.

## Italian Pasta Bolognese

*Ingredients*
2 tablespoons butter
1/4 pound sliced bacon, cut crosswise into 1/4-
   inch strips
1 onion, chopped
1/2 pound ground beef
1 cup canned low-sodium chicken broth
1/2 cup dry white wine
2 tablespoons tomato paste
1/2 teaspoon dried oregano
3/4 teaspoons salt
1/4 teaspoon fresh ground black pepper
1/2 cup heavy cream
3/4 pound spaghetti
2 tablespoons fresh parsley, chopped

*Directions*
In a large frying pan, heat the butter and bacon over moderately low heat. Fry for about 3 minutes, or until the bacon has rendered much of its fat. Add the onion and saute, stirring occasionally, until it begins to soften, about 3 minutes longer. Stir in the ground beef and cook just until the meat is no longer pink. Add the broth, wine, tomato paste, oregano, salt, and pepper. Simmer uncovered, stirring occasionally, until the sauce thickens, about 25 minutes. Stir in the cream and remove from the heat.

   In a large pot of boiling, salted water, cook the spaghetti until just done, about 12 minutes. Drain and toss with the sauce and the parsley.

## Pasta Fagiole

*Ingredients*
1 pound ditalini or other small pasta shape
1/4 cup olive oil
1 clove garlic, finely minced
2 large green peppers, chopped
1 cup chopped onions
1 cup chopped celery
1 16-ounce can tomato puree
1 can water
salt and freshly ground black pepper to taste
dash of dried parsley
2 12-ounce cans white cannelini beans

*Directions*
Prepare pasta according to package directions, drain.

   While pasta is cooking, heat oil in large saucepan. Add garlic, green pepper, onions, and celery, and sauté until tender. Add tomato puree and water, and seasonings. Cook on low for 30 minutes. Add beans and stir. Add bean mixture to pasta. Mix well and serve.

## Patate e Cipolle (Potatoes and Onions)

*Ingredients*
2 pounds potatoes
2 pounds onions
extra virgin olive oil
fresh rosemary
salt

*Directions*
Preheat oven to 350°F.

Wash and peel onions and potatoes. Cut each into 1/2-inch slices. In an ovenproof dish, alternate layers of potatoes and onions. Season with the oil, rosemary, and salt. Bake in preheated oven for 30 minutes, or until potatoes are crispy and golden. Serve warm.

## Rotolo di Spinaci (Spinach Roll)

Serves 6–8

*Ingredients*
For the dough:
3 cups all purpose flour
3 tablespoon extra virgin olive oil
pinch of salt
lukewarm water as needed

For the filling:
1 pound and 9 ounces fresh spinach
1 medium onion, finely chopped
1 garlic clove
3 tablespoons extra virgin olive oil
5 ounces Asiago cheese chopped
salt to taste
pinch of nutmeg

*Directions*
First, prepare the dough. In a medium bowl, combine the flour, oil, water, and salt. Knead the dough until smooth, and set aside, covered, for 30 minutes.

To prepare the filling, heat the oil in a nonstick pan. Add the onions and sauté until translucent, being careful not to burn.

Thoroughly wash the spinach in running cold water. In a large saucepan, boil the spinach in salted water for 2 minutes. Drain well. Place the cooked spinach in a clean kitchen towel and squeeze out the excess water.

(You can also run it through a salad spinner.) Finely chop the drained spinach. Combine the spinach, onions, nutmeg, and salt, and place in a bowl. Allow to cool, then add the Asiago cheese. Set aside.

On a clean kitchen towel or a sheet of parchment paper, roll out the dough in a rectangular shape until very thin. Spread the filling evenly on the dough. Fold in the shorter sides. Using the kitchen towel or parchment paper, roll the dough up like a jelly roll. Place in a baking dish and brush with olive oil. Preheat the oven to 375°F, and bake for 30 to 40 minutes.

Cut into slices and serve warm.

# PROJECT AND REPORT IDEAS

## Maps

- Using a map of modern-day Italy and a key containing the names of Italian cities, see how many classmates can point out correctly the important Italian cities of Rome, Venice, Naples, Turin, and Milan. Also see who can correctly identify the islands of Sardinia and Sicily.
- Make a map of Italy and indicate the major cities and geographical features.

## Reports

- Write a report on the history of Christianity and its foundations in Rome.
- Write a report about the eruption of Mount Vesuvius and the city of Pompeii.
- Imagine you are a reporter, and write an article about one of the major events in Italian history.

## Biographies

Using the Internet and textbooks as sources, write a biography on one of the following:
- Julius Caesar
- Michelangelo
- Machiavelli
- Benito Mussolini

## Journal

- Imagine you are a teenager during the rule of Mussolini. Write a journal telling what life is like.

## Projects

- Bring in examples of Renaissance art, and give a brief presentation about Italian artists of the period.
- Make a model of a volcano.

## Group Activities

- Debate: One side argues for returning the lire as the national monetary unit. The other side argues for retaining the use of the euro.
- Make the recipes from this book and elsewhere, and have a "food fest."

# CHRONOLOGY

| | |
|---|---|
| 753 BCE | According to legend, twins Romulus and Remus found Rome. |
| 509 BCE | The Roman Republic begins. |
| 340–338 BCE | Rome and its Latin kinsmen battle for the right to dominate Latium. |
| 334–264 BCE | Rome begins to spread its colonial influence to the rest of the Italian Peninsula; Rome begins to mint coins. |
| 289–275 BCE | Roman goes to war with Pyrrhus. |
| 241 BCE | Sicily is made a Roman province. |
| 238 BCE | Sardinia and Corsica are made Roman provinces. |
| 49–44 BCE | Julius Caesar becomes head of Roman Republic; he is assassinated in 44 BCE. |
| 27 BCE | Augustus Caesar becomes emperor of Rome. |
| 43 CE | Romans occupy Britannia (Britain). |
| 79 | Mount Vesuvius erupts, burying the ancient city of Pompeii in ash. |
| 313 | Roman emperor Constantine declares Christianity the official religion of the empire and ends persecution of Christians. |
| 476 | Rome falls. |
| 773–774 | Charlemagne conquers Italy. |
| 827 | Arabs invade Sicily, and capture the island in 902. |
| 1061–1091 | Normans conquer Italy. |
| 1252 | First gold coins minted in Europe are made in Florence. |
| 1348–1349 | The Black Plague ravages Italy. |
| 1378 | The Great Schism begins. |
| 1414–1418 | The Council of Constance ends the Great Schism. |
| 1452 | Leonardo da Vinci is born in Anchiano, Italy. |
| 1508–1512 | Michelangelo paints the ceiling of the Sistine Chapel. |
| 1633 | Astronomer and scientist Galileo is condemned in Rome. |
| 1861 | The Kingdom of Italy is founded with King Emmanuel II of Sardinia as king. |
| 1911–1912 | Italy conquers Libya. |
| 1915 | Italy enters World War I on the side of the Allies. |
| 1922 | Mussolini is named prime minister of Italy; fascist rule begins. |
| 1940 | Italy enters World War II on the side of the Axis. |
| 1944 | The Allies take Rome. |
| 1945 | World War II ends. |
| 1946 | The monarchy is abolished, and the Republic of Italy is formed. |
| 1949 | Italy joins NATO. |
| 2001 | Silvio Berlusconi becomes prime minister of Italy. |

# FURTHER READING/INTERNET RESOURCES

Bisignano, Alphonse. *Cooking the Italian Way.* Minneapolis, Minn.: Lerner Publishing Group, 2001.
Koelihoffer, Tara. *The History of Nations: Italy.* Farmington Hills, Mich.: Thomson Gale, 2003.
Marston, Elsa. *The Byzantine Empire.* New York: Benchmark Books, 2002.
Pavlovic, Zoran. *Italy.* Northborough, Mass.: Chelsea House, 2003.

## Travel Information
www.italiantourism.com
www.italy-travel-information.com
www.touritalynow.com

## History and Geography
www.arcaini.com/ITALY/ItalyHistory/ItalyHistory.html
workmall.com/wfb2001/italy/italy_history_index.html

## Culture and Festivals
www.globalvolunteers.org/1main/italy/italyculture.htm
www.hostetler.net/italy/italy.cfm
www.justitaly.org/italy/italy-festivals.asp

## Economic and Political Information
www.cia.gov/cia/publications/factbook/geos/it.html

## EU Information
europa.eu.int

# FOR MORE INFORMATION

Embassy of Italy
3000 Whitehaven Street NW
Washington, DC 20008
Tel.: 202-612-4400
Fax: 202-518-2154

Embassy of the United States
via Vittorio Veneto 119/A
00187 Roma, Italia
Tel.: 39-06-4674-1

European Union
Delegation of the European Commission to the United States
2300 M Street NW
Washington, DC 20037
Tel.: 202-862-9500
Fax: 202-429-1766

Permanent Mission of Italy to the United Nations
2 United Nations Plaza, 24th Floor
New York, NY 10017
Tel.: 646-840-5300
e-mail: italy@un.int.

U.S. Department of State
2201 C Street NW
Washington, DC 20520
Tel.: 202-642-4000

# GLOSSARY

**annexed:** Took over a territory and incorporated it into another political entity.

**appease:** To pacify someone, especially by giving in to demands.

**autonomous:** Politically independent and self-governing.

**bicameral:** Having two separate lawmaking assemblies.

**blocs:** United groups of countries.

**capital:** Wealth in the form of property or money.

**castigation:** The act of criticizing, rebuking, or punishing someone severely.

**censured:** Expressed official disapproval.

**city-states:** Independent states consisting of a sovereign city and its surrounding territory.

**encroaching:** Gradually intruding.

**excise:** A government-imposed tax on domestic goods.

**frescoes:** Paintings done on ceilings or walls in watercolor on fresh, damp plaster.

**gastronomic:** Relating to the art and appreciation of preparing and eating good food.

**gross domestic product (GDP):** The total value of all goods and services produced in a country in a year, minus net income from investments in other countries.

**icon:** A picture that symbolizes something else.

**indigenous:** Native to an area.

**Marshall Plan:** A program of loans and other economic assistance provided by the U.S. government between 1947 and 1952 to help western European nations rebuild after World War II.

**Neolithic:** The latest period of the Stone Age, approximately 8000 BCE to 5000 BCE.

**opulent:** Characterized by an obvious, lavish display of wealth.

**papacy:** Relating to the government of the Roman Catholic Church, headed by the pope.

**prehistoric:** Before the time when history was recorded in written form.

**proponent:** Someone in favor of something.

**quelled:** Brought something to an end, often by force.

**ratified:** Officially approved.

**republic:** A form of government in which people elect representatives to vote on their behalf.

**Romance language:** A language that has descended from Latin.

**satiate:** To satisfy a hunger completely.

**service sector:** Businesses that sell a service rather than a product.

**Shroud of Turin:** A burial cloth believed by some to have covered the body of Jesus Christ.

**solidarity:** Standing united.

**stagnancy:** A period of inactivity.

**suffrage:** The right to vote.

**tariff:** A government-imposed tax on imports.

**truffles:** A highly prized, edible, underground fungus.

# INDEX

# PICTURE CREDITS

# BIOGRAPHIES

## AUTHOR

Nigerian-born Ademola Sadik first visited Italy as a young child en route to Australia, where he and his family resided for several years. Future relocations would lead him to Las Vegas and finally to Upstate New York. With several members of his family living in Italy, Ademola contacts them via phone and Internet on a semiregular basis.

## SERIES CONSULTANTS

Ambassador John Bruton served as Irish Prime Minister from 1994 until 1997. As prime minister, he helped turn Ireland's economy into one of the fastest-growing in the world. He was also involved in the Northern Ireland Peace Process, which led to the 1998 Good Friday Agreement. During his tenure as Ireland's prime minister, he also presided over the European Union presidency in 1996 and helped finalize the Stability and Growth Pact, which governs management of the euro. Before being named the European Commission Head of Delegation in the United States, he was a member of the convention that drafted the European Constitution, signed October 29, 2004.

The European Commission Delegation to the United States represents the interests of the European Union as a whole, much as ambassadors represent their countries' interests to the U.S. government. Matters coming under European Commission authority are negotiated between the commission and the U.S. administration.